Financial Economics:

A Simple Introduction

Also by K.H. Erickson

<u>Simple Introductions</u>

Choice Theory
Financial Economics
Game Theory
Game Theory for Business
Investment Appraisal
Microeconomics

Financial Economics:

A Simple Introduction

K.H. Erickson

© 2013 K.H. Erickson

All rights reserved.

No part of this publication may be reproduced, stored in or introduced into a retrieval system, or transmitted in any form or by any means, including electronic, mechanical, photocopying, recording or otherwise, without the prior permission of the author.

Contents

1 Introduction	6
2 Consumption and Investment	9
2.1 Intertemporal Choice	9
2.2 Production Possibility Frontier	14
2.3 Borrowing and Lending	20
2.4 Fisher Separation Theorem	26
3 Portfolio Theory	33
3.1 Risk and Return	33
3.2 Portfolio Diversification	37
3.3 A Risk-Free Asset	49
3.4 Market Portfolio and Capital Market Line	55
4 Capital Asset Pricing Model (CAPM)	58
4.1 Systematic Risk	58
4.2 CAPM Assumptions and Expression	60
4.3 Security Market Line and Asset Valuation	63
4.4 Empirical Evidence on the CAPM	74
5 Market Efficiency	78
5.1 Efficient Market Hypothesis	78
5.2 Beating the Market	84
5.3 Weak Form Market Analysis	86
5.4 Semi-Strong Form Market Analysis	90
5.5 Strong Form Market Analysis	94
Bibliography	96

1 Introduction

Financial economics is concerned with the allocation of resources in an uncertain environment, with a focus on monetary activities involving the trade of one form of money for another form, and on financial markets in particular. The subject area incorporates decision making at all levels, from uninformed consumers to qualified investment experts, market researchers and analysts, and the countless individuals who together bring about the self-adjusting market valuation system.

Consumption and investment is the first area to be examined and individuals are faced with intertemporal choice, as they allocate consumption over time and invest the income that remains. Indifference curves and the marginal rate of substitution are introduced, to determine how an individual would like to divide consumption between now and the future, before the production possibility frontier shows the limits of consumption and the marginal rate of transformation between consumption over time. A third element is added with the financial market line, which allows borrowing or lending of wealth between periods, and calculations are shown to move between future and present value. In certain conditions there may be complete separation between the consumption choice and investment decision, known as the Fisher Separation Theorem, but if these conditions break down then individuals are revealed to face a suboptimal outcome.

Investment is looked at in-depth with an examination of portfolio theory. Expected return, standard deviation risk and variance are added to the discussion, along with the mathematical formulas used to calculate them. The main focal point of the topic is the gains on offer from portfolio diversification, and numerical examples and diagrams show how a well diversified portfolio can reduce risk without sacrificing the expected return. A risk-free asset is introduced with the market portfolio on the capital market line, and they're revealed to be an essential part of an equilibrium portfolio.

The capital asset pricing model (CAPM) is the focus of the next section, as investors must price assets to deal with non-diversifiable risk. This model combines the risk-free rate and market portfolio to find another efficient market line, as the security market line measures the expected return against beta risk, which represents the sensitivity of an asset to market changes. Numerical examples are given to calculate the expected return of an asset if the other factors are known, and also to estimate beta in a range of scenarios. Assets may not necessarily place on the security market line, potentially sitting below or above it as overvalued or undervalued stocks, and this can challenge the entire validity of the CAPM as an asset valuation tool. Empirical evidence on the strengths and weaknesses of the model ends the section.

The final topic turns to the question of market efficiency, which is central to the idea of efficient market lines and market portfolios throughout financial economics. An efficient market hypothesis is put forward with the idea that prices follow a random walk, and this is separated into weak, semi-strong and strong levels of efficiency, but professional analysts may work on the basis that markets are inefficient, and the methods they may use to gain excess returns are outlined. An extensive analysis is then made on weak, semi-strong and strong form levels of market efficiency, using research from others to summarize the empirical evidence and draw conclusions on the state of the market.

2 Consumption and Investment

2.1 Intertemporal Choice

The ways that firms and individuals allocate resources through time is a central focus in financial economics, and the field is known more broadly as intertemporal choice. Capital markets are an essential part of this process, and they allow individuals to exchange resources available at one period in time for resources at another time, while the production or investment decisions of firms transform current physical assets into future resources.

A sum of money could be invested in a five year fixed rate savings account today, and in five years a larger sum of money would be available to replace it. Alternatively, a small business might convince a lender that it has a strong business plan that would generate big returns in the future, and receive a loan in the present to make it happen. At the physical level firms invest in creating buildings and institutions, and train individuals to provide a lifelong resource stream in return.

To model the consumption and investment decision in the wider economy some simplifications have to be made, and it's useful to imagine a single representative individual who has a choice whether to consume or invest in a single good. The one person, one good model sees the individual decide how much to consume now and how much to invest in the future. These are the only two options, and a decision not to consume now is equivalent to a decision to invest. To develop the model into a predictive tool further simplifying assumptions are useful:

1) No taxes and no transaction costs;
2) Decision is for one period only, and events occur at its start or end;
3) Y0 income is received at the start of the period, and Y1 income is received at the end of the period;
4) Returns outcome from investment is known with certainty;
5) Marginal utility (MU) of consumption is positive, and an incremental increase in consumption is beneficial;
6) MU of consumption falls as consumption increases.

These assumptions allow some conclusions to be drawn about the individual's preferences. He will be indifferent between certain combinations of consumption shared between the start and end of a period which lasts for one year, and willing to delay current consumption for a certain amount that will occur in the future. The individual's preferences are given by his marginal rate of substitution (MRS) between consumption at the beginning (C0) and end of the period (C1). This is found by dividing the change in C1 ($\Delta C1$) by the change in C0 ($\Delta C0$), and adding a negative sign to account for having to give up some current consumption:

$$MRS = - (\Delta C1 / \Delta C0)$$

For example, if the individual was willing to give up 10 units of consumption at the beginning of the period, as long as he received 12 units of consumption at the end, MRS = - (12 / -10) = 1.2. The individual would substitute 1 unit of consumption now for a rate of 1.2 units later.

The preferences of an individual can be shown in an indifference curve, where the slope determines the marginal rate of substitution (MRS), and this is affected by the rate of return on investment (RI):

$$MRS = - (1 + RI)$$

A typical indifference curve is shown below, with changing slopes and investment rates of return at different points, given by the two tangent lines of MRS 1 and MRS 2. These show the individual's changing MRS and subjective rate of time preference for consumption, which falls with a move down the curve. An individual will be indifferent between any points on this curve, and any point gives as much utility and satisfaction as another.

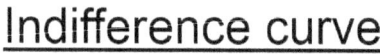

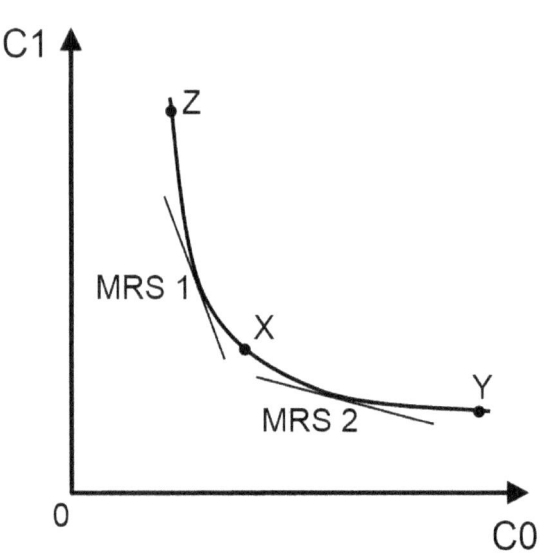

Those who have never seen an indifference curve before may wonder why indifference is represented by a curve, and not a straight line. This is because of the idea of declining marginal utility of consumption, where there are diminishing returns as the utility gained from one good falls as consumption rises, although it remains positive.

The individual here would gain a good level of utility if consumption were divided equally between both now and at the end of period next year, at the most curved point of the indifference curve at point X. But if almost all of his consumption was now, C0, at point Y, then diminishing returns would set in and it would take more total consumption to satisfy him and get the same level of utility, and the same holds if almost all consumption was set to occur next year, C1, at point Z. Greater total consumption (C0 + C1) clearly occurs at points Y and Z than at point X, and for X to involve the same amount of total consumption it would have to have been situated on a straight line between Y and Z. But by combining consumption now and later in a certain amount at point X the individual gains the same utility as at Y and Z, without having to engage in as much (usually costly) consumption as would otherwise be required.

2.2 Production Possibility Frontier

After looking at consumption the next step is to look into the investment opportunities that are available. As before C0 and C1 represent the consumption at the start and end of the period respectively, while Y0 and Y1 refer to the income at the start and end, and RI the rate of return on investment. One other factor added is the investment at the start of the period (I0). The relationship between the various factors can be given with the following equation:

$$C1 = Y1 + I0 (1 + RI)$$

In other words, consumption at the period end (C1) equals income at the period end (Y1) and the total returns from investment, where the total return equals the amount invested at the beginning of the period (I0 (1)) added to the amount generated at a certain rate of return (I0 (RI)).

To represent example investment opportunities the various factors need to be given values. The start and end period levels of income, Y0 and Y1, will be fixed: Y0 = £1,000; Y1 = £500.

Consumption at the beginning of the time period, C0, will be given a range of values rising in £100 steps from £0 to £1,000 (the maximum possible with Y0 starting income): C0 = £0; £100, £200, £300, £400; £500; £600;

£700; £800; £900; 1,000. And the investment at the start of the period, I0, will simply be however much start of period income (Y0 = £1,000) is not consumed right away at the start: I0 = £1,000 - C0.

But the rate of return will depend on the amount invested, and in a world of limited productive investment opportunities the rate of return may fall for ever greater investment levels: RI = 10% for 1st £100 invested; RI = 9% for 2nd £100 invested; RI = 8% for 3rd £100 invested; RI = 7% for 4th £100 invested; RI = 6% for 5th £100 invested; RI = 5% for 6th £100 invested; RI = 4% for 7th £100 invested; RI = 3% for 8th £100 invested; RI = 2% for 9th £100 invested; RI = 1% for 10th £100 invested.

All of the above information can be used to create a table that gives the possible values of C0, C1, I0, and I0 (1 + RI), depending on how the representative individual decides to allocate consumption and investment over time:

C0	I0	I0 (1 + RI)	C1
1000	0	0	500
900	100	100 (1.1)	610
800	200	100 (1.1) + 100 (1.09) = 21.9	719
700	300	327	827
600	400	434	934
500	500	540	1040
400	600	645	1145
300	700	749	1249
200	800	852	1352
100	900	954	1454
0	1000	1055	1555

The general trend shown by the data can be put into a simplifying diagram form. This represents the range of investment and consumption opportunities on offer to the individual, and is called a production possibility frontier (PPF).

Production possibility frontier

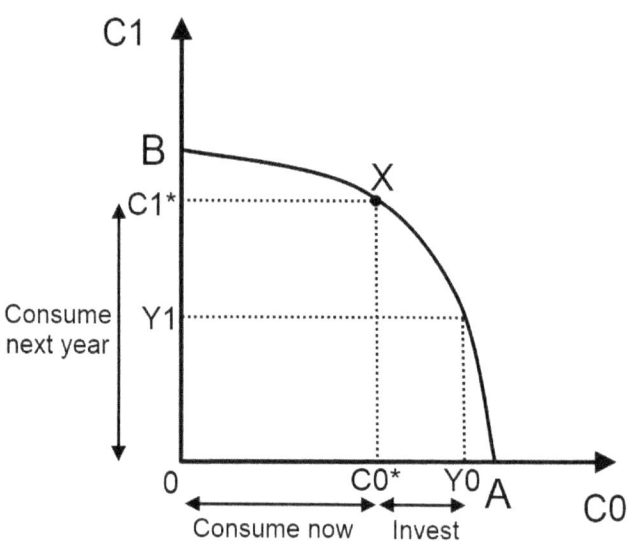

The diagram is not to scale but it shows the general form and trend of consumption and investment opportunities. The slope of the PPF changes with a movement from consumption now to consumption in the future, similar to the indifference curve seen in the previous section above, and this is again due to the idea of diminishing returns which holds for both investment and consumption. But here the PPF curve bends outwards and not inwards, as while an indifference curve shows the least required (for a certain level of utility), the PPF curve shows the highest possible (production).

At point A there is maximum possible consumption at the start of the period, C0, and all start period income, Y0 = £1,000, is spent on consumption now, C0 = £1,000. At the other end of the scale at point B there's full investment and no consumption now, C0 = £0, and this allows resources to be put toward the maximum possible consumption at the end of the period next year, C1.

Point X also represents another point of maximum possible consumption on the boundary of the production possibility frontier, except this time the consumption is divided between both now, C0, and at the end of the period, C1. At point X the individual consumes amount C0* now, with the remaining start period income going toward a decision to invest, C0* + I0 = Y0 = £1,000. This decision on consumption and investment now allows the individual to consume level C1* next year.

Finally, the point where Y0 and Y1 meet shows the result of dedicating all income to consumption as soon as it is received, whether at the start or the end of the period.

While the tangent of an indifference curve slope gives the marginal rate of substitution (MRS), the tangent of a PPF curve gives the marginal rate of transformation

(MRT). It reveals how foregone consumption today is transformed into consumption in the future. The MRS shows how an individual would like to exchange consumption now for that in the future, and the MRT shows how the individual could exchange current consumption for future consumption.

Combining indifference curve preferences with production possibilities shows what to expect in the division of consumption and investment, and the solution occurs where MRS = MRT at point X. This point determines the consumption level now, C0, consumption next year, C1, and the size of the investment, I0.

Consumption and investment

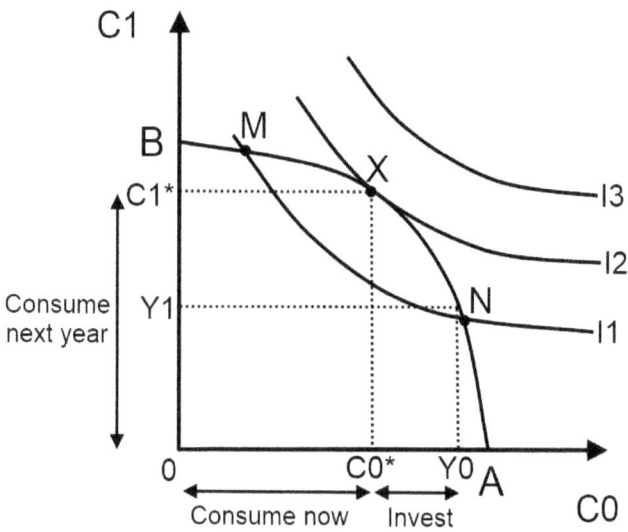

In the amended diagram three indifference curves have been added, showing the various combinations of current and future consumption for which the individual holds the same preferences. But while he is indifferent to the position he sits upon a particular indifference curve, he strongly prefers to be on a separate higher curve than a lower one for the greater utility.

Here the lowest indifference curve is I1, but although this crosses the PPF at points M and N the individual will ignore this and search out a higher indifference curve, I2. This curve offers higher consumption both now, C0, and in the future, C1, than curve I1, and it offers increased utility as a result. Higher curve I3 would be even better, but unfortunately for the individual it doesn't cross the PPF and there's no point where MRS = MRT, and the opportunities available match his preferences. As a result the indifference curve I2 is the one that's chosen as MRS = MRT at point X, and the individual will invest from this point as the diagram shows.

2.3 Borrowing and Lending

With the consumption and investment decision found for a single representative individual the focus can return to the wider economy, where the presence of other individuals allows for the possibility of exchange of intertemporal consumption between them. For simplicity it's assumed that:

1) There are fully efficient perfect capital markets, where all traders have equal and zero-cost access to information;

2) Both buyers and sellers are price-takers who are forced to accept the going price;

3) No transfer taxes, transaction costs or brokerage fees.

These conditions allow individuals to borrow or lend money at the market rate of interest (r).

An individual's wealth at the start of a period, W_0, will be his current income, Y_0, and his future income to be achieved at the end of the period, Y_1, adjusted to its present value. This future income has to be included as it is guaranteed income that affects the wealth level, but it needs to be converted from its future value (e.g. £210 to be received next year) to its reduced present value to show its true worth.

£210 today is worth more than £210 in the future, and if received now it could be loaned out to others with e.g. a 5% market rate of interest, and a year from now £210 would have transformed into:

$$210*(1 + 0.05) = 210*1.05 = £220.50$$

To find out how much £210 received next year is worth today the process is simply reversed:

$$210 / (1 + 0.05) = 210 / 1.05 = £200$$

Bearing this in mind an equation can be formed to find current wealth, $W0$:

$$W0 = Y0 + Y1 / (1 + r)$$

And it's also possible to find future wealth, $W1$, at the end of the period a year from now. It will simply be current wealth, $W0$, with an addition to represent the market rate of interest:

$$W1 = W0(1 + r) + Y0(1 + r) + Y1$$

With both the wealth at the start and end of the period, $W0$ and $W1$, a diagram can show how this affects the decision on the level of consumption. The start and end period wealth give the financial market line (FML), which determines the maximum amount of money that an individual could lend or borrow.

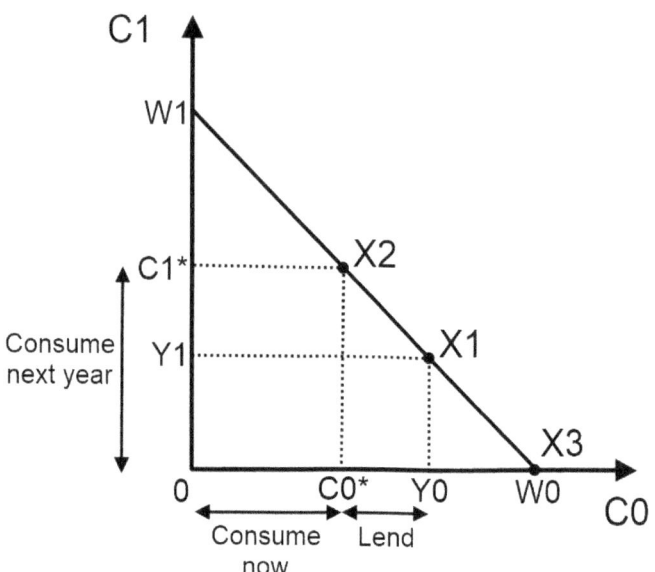

The point W0 shows the individual's current wealth, which is current income, Y0, and the present value of future wealth. W0 shows the maximum possible consumption available now if all resources went toward current consumption, C0. W1 shows the maximum possible consumption if all resources were put to future consumption at the end of the period next year, and all points between W0 and W1 represent the financial market line, with all of the possible combinations of maximum consumption divided between the start and end of the period.

An individual could choose to consume all of his current income, Y0, and all of his future income, Y1, when he gets it, and make no attempt to lend or borrow. This would give outcome X1 on the financial market line, with the combination of current and future consumption shown. Alternatively he could consume less than all of his current income now, for example at level C0*, and point X2 on the FML shows the level of future consumption this would allow, at C1*. The remainder of current income, Y0 - C0*, could be loaned out to others at the market rate of interest. Finally there is a third option, and the individual could not only consume all of his current wealth now, but also use the present value of his future wealth as collateral to borrow more from financial institutions, which he would then consume today. This occurs at point X3, and there's maximum consumption today on the C0 axis, but 0 at the end of the period on the C1 axis.

With a range of opportunities given by the financial market line a choice must be made between whether to borrow, lend, or neither. The decision made will depend on the utility derived from each option, and which of the three puts the individual on the highest available indifference curve.

Borrowing and lending preferences

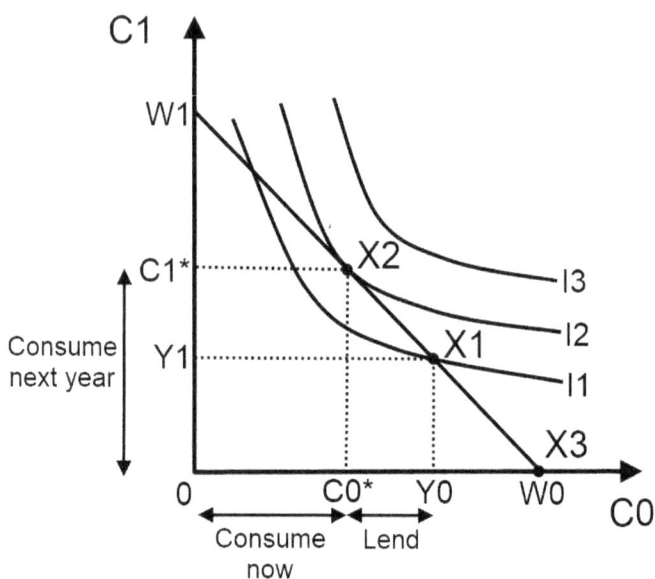

If the individual were to borrow to consume all of his current wealth now (both current income and the present value of future income) he would be at point X3. This point is below the three indifference curves shown here and is therefore a suboptimal choice. Alternatively he may neither borrow nor lend and simply consume his current income, and this would see him at point X1 on indifference curve I1, with greater utility than borrowing can offer. But if the individual only consumed at a level of C0* and loaned out what remained of his current income,

Y0 - C0*, he would be at point X2 on indifference curve I2. This offers a higher level of utility than the other two options and is what the individual can be expected to choose. Indifference curve I3 is the highest shown in the diagram and the individual would prefer to be on this curve most of all, but that isn't an option here due to the position of the financial market line. For an investor to reach I3 his wealth would have to increase to see the FML move tangent to this preference curve.

2.4 Fisher Separation Theorem

The diagrams above have shown the preferred outcome for a person when indifference curves are combined with the production possibility frontier, and separately when indifference curves are combined with the financial market line and the market rate of interest to show their possible wealth. But to get the complete picture of how an individual will decide to consume or invest requires consumption preferences, production, and the wealth available with market borrowing or lending to be combined into one diagram.

In the following diagram W0, W1 is the financial market line as before (dashed for clarity to avoid confusion with the other lines and curves) based on the market rate of interest, the curve between 'A' and 'B' is the production possibility frontier (PPF), and the indifference curves show an individual's preferences for consumption now (C0) and consumption next year (C1). In previous diagrams the equilibrium outcome was where an individual's highest indifference curve met the PPF and MRS = MRT, or where the highest indifference curve met the financial market line, W0 to W1. That remains the case here too except in this diagram there are two separate outcomes, and point X2 gives optimal production, while point X1 is optimal consumption given wealth constraints.

Utility, PPF and FML combined

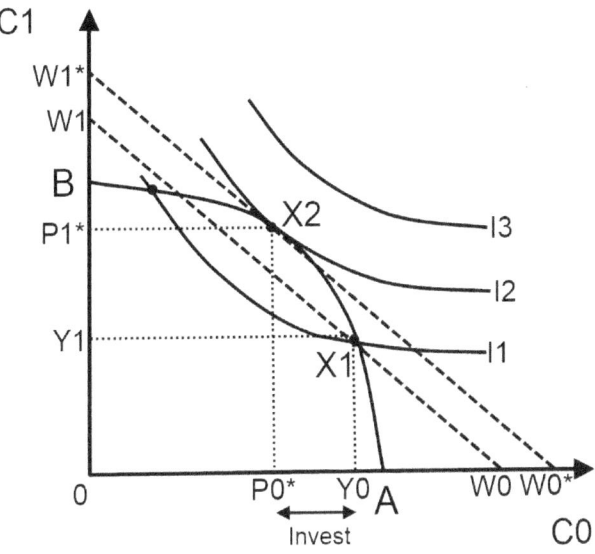

Previous diagrams have already shown that the subjective rate of time preference for the individual is where the PPF is tangent to his highest possible indifference curve, point X2 on indifference curve I2. He would like current consumption at level C0* with price P0*, and end of period consumption at level C1* with price P1*. But as the diagram above shows this point lies beyond the financial market line, W0 to W1, and isn't achievable at current wealth levels. Therefore a decision is made to forget about future consumption for the moment, and choose current consumption C0* at price P0*, and invest (i.e. lend) the remainder of current income Y0 until all remaining current wealth is invested out at the market rate of interest, at the W0 to W1 line. This consumption strategy sees an outcome of point X1, on the highest available indifference curve I1.

Point X1 lies on the PPF, the production possibility frontier, and the individual's decision to invest allows him to move along the PPF from point X1 to point X2 where productive opportunities offer a superior return in excess of the market rate of interest. These investment opportunities generate increased wealth in the future at W1*, and the present value of this is W0*, to see the financial market line expands for this now wealthier individual. The higher indifference curve I2 is available at this point, as is the preferred level of end period consumption, C1* at price P1*.

With all of the factors in the consumption and investment decision together, it's clear there are two separate steps in an individual's decision-making process:

The optimal level of production is given by investment in opportunities with a higher rate of return than the market interest rate. This is the investment decision;

The optimal level of consumption is achieved by borrowing or lending up to the point where an individual's subjective rate of time preference equals the market rate of interest. This is the consumption decision.

This separation of the decision-making process into two distinct steps for consumption and investment is known as the Fisher Separation Theorem (FST), or alternatively as the Hirshleifer Separation Theorem. The FST has some significant implications, and investment decisions are independent of both ownership and financing, with the wealth owner's unique consumption preferences and financing strategy of borrowing or lending completely irrelevant to optimal investment.

Because the investor's preferences don't have an impact on the investment decision the process can be designated to external managers. This is the foundation upon which modern financial institutions are built, and financial experts can invest on the behalf of their investors without the latter having to worry that their goals aren't being met. The subjective rate of time preference and marginal rate of substitution (MRS) for an individual doesn't affect the optimal investment, and multiple different investors with varying MRS will have the same investment decision, where the marginal rate of transformation (MRT) for production is tangent with the financial market line of wealth:

$$MRS1 = MRS2 = MRT = - (1 + r)$$

This equilibrium can be seen below, where $W0^*$ to $W1^*$ has become the new wealth level and financial market line, and MRS 1 would represent the marginal rate of substitution for a lender, and MRS 2 for a borrower.

Fisher separation theorem

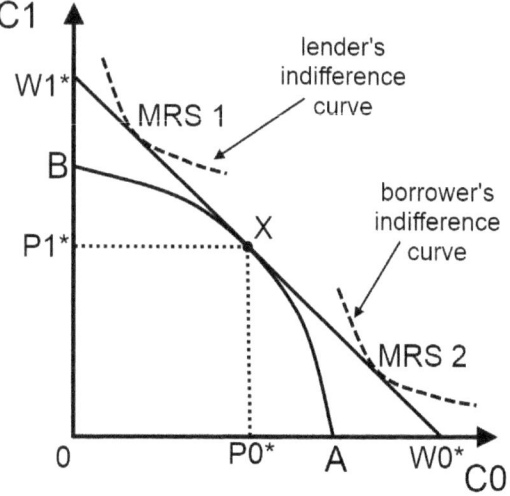

Point X shows the point where MRT = - (1 + r) and this will be the investment decision for all investors, and managers working for them. The equilibrium occurs where MRS = MRT and both MRS 1 and MRS 2 have the same slope as MRT here. MRS 1 belongs to a lender and he will consume levels of C0 and C1 at this point, and lend/invest what remains of his current wealth to move right along the financial market line (FML) to point X. MRS 2 could belong to the borrower who takes the lender's money, and he consumes a level of current consumption beyond his wealth made possible by the loan, as his investment moves leftwards along the FML to point X. Borrowing and lending at the market rate make all of this possible.

But the entire system of separating investor preferences from investment decisions depends on one market rate of interest, to allow all borrowers and lenders to move from their subjective consumption optimum to the optimal point for production. With two different market rates of interest, such as a high rate for borrowers to exploit their position of need, and a low rate for lenders to take their money without giving much back in return, the entire Fisher separation theorem (FST) will break down.

Fisher separation theorem breakdown

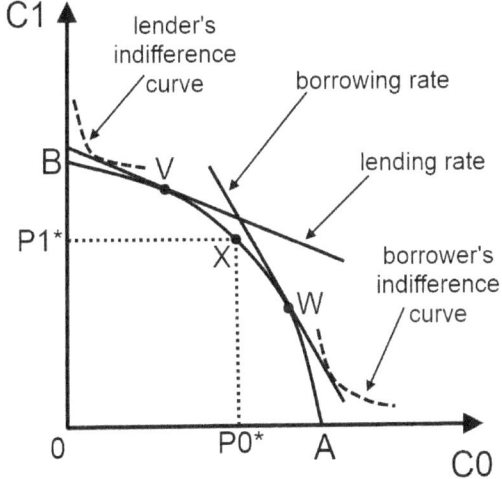

Point X is the optimal production and investment decision, but with separate rates for lending and borrowing here neither a lender nor a borrower can reach it, and there's no single financial market line. The best a lender following the lending rate can achieve is point V, a sub-optimal point, while the most a borrower could hope for with the borrowing rate is point W, also sub-optimal. Neither rate allows the lender or borrower achieve the superior investment they would desire, and this sees the FST collapse as both lenders and borrowers know they can't separate consumption and investment decisions. They would need to position themselves at one point in the previous diagram, and either give up on the optimal investment of point X or abandon their preferred level of consumption. They would most likely choose the former.

Not only is a breakdown of the FST bad for individual investors, it's also bad for the economy as a whole. Inefficiency is created by investors being unable to achieve both optimal consumption and investment, and having to spend the time to make investment decisions themselves instead of being able to designate it to others. A properly functioning financial sector is an essential foundation for an efficient and productive economy, and a single market rate of interest to support the FST is a crucial part of this. But it's only one part of the system, and even if the FST holds and the investment decision can be designated to finance managers, they still must do their job properly. This is the focus of the next section.

3 Portfolio Theory

3.1 Risk and Return

The investment decision has a simple goal: to achieve the maximum possible return and maximize returns. A good measure of the monetary return is the mean or expected value associated with the investment returns, which weights each outcome against its probability or proportional impact (P). A portfolio could contain two assets, asset 1 and asset 2. An individual invests in the two assets so that asset 1 makes up proportion P1 in the portfolio, and asset 2 makes up the remaining proportion P2. If asset 1 offers expected return E(R1), and asset 2 expected return E(R2), then the expected return of the portfolio, E(Rp), can be found:

$$E(Rp) = P1*E(R1) + P2*E(R2)$$

For example, if an investment portfolio contained two different assets in equal amount then each would represent a 50% proportion of the portfolio. And if asset 1 gave a 6% return after one year, while asset 2 gave a 12% return after the same time period, the expected return of the complete portfolio, E(Rp), could be calculated:

$$E(R) = (0.5)*0.06 + (0.5)*0.12$$
$$E(R) = 0.03 + 0.06$$
$$E(R) = 0.09 \text{ or } 9\%$$

In this example the portfolio of two assets could be expected to give a return of 9% after one year. And the manager could remove the first asset and fill up his portfolio with the second one, to then secure a superior 12% return in a one asset portfolio.

But unfortunately for portfolio managers it's not usually as easy as just picking the asset with the highest return and watching the money roll in. Risk plays a big part and there are often several possible outcomes, more than will actually occur, and no-one can be sure which will happen. The expected return is one important piece of information and it gives the mean return, but investors will also be concerned with the dispersion of possible returns around this mean. Investors are typically risk averse in their investment decisions, and are concerned about the risk of a return lower than the expected mean, instead of welcoming the linked prospect of a potentially excess return that outperforms it. This creates a risk-return trade-off, where investors want to maximize the return and minimize the risk.

In the situation where there's a normal distribution of returns the best measure of dispersion will either be the standard deviation (SD), or the variance (Var). Calculation of the variance follows a similar formula to that of the expected return, except the individual return in the formula is replaced by the difference between the return (R) and the expected mean return (E(R)), and then squared:

$$\text{Variance} = E(R - E(R))^2$$

And the standard deviation is the square root of the variance:

$$SD = E(R - E(R))$$

As the variance is the square of the SD it may be written as SD^2 in shorthand. The variance and standard deviation will always be positive numbers and they can never be negative. Squaring the factors in brackets ensures this for the variance, and a square root of a positive number is also positive to see it hold for SD.

With a normal distribution, as is the default and usually well founded assumption for all data sets, the mean and standard deviation describe the distribution completely, giving the risk and return for an investment. The only question is how investors use the information to choose between investment alternatives.

If two different investments have the same expected rate of return but one has higher risk, then the other one with lower risk will be preferred. If two different investments have the same risk but one has a higher expected return, then that one will be preferred. But an investor having a preference means nothing, and what matters is whether or not the preferred asset will be chosen in the investment decision, and included in the portfolio. And that decision depends on what the considered asset will add to the portfolio, relative to the other assets already chosen.

It may be the case that holding a diversified portfolio with a different range of investments reduces the variance and risk. This seems intuitive and common sense, as suggested by the expression 'don't put all your eggs in one basket.' For example, holding two property stocks in a two asset portfolio could put the entire portfolio at risk in the event that the property market suffered a downturn, but holding one property stock and one non-property stock would reduce the risk of this problem. Therefore it's not just the mean and variance that would matter to investors, as the covariance of the assets could potentially have a big impact on portfolio risk. But before choosing to diversify assets in a portfolio the theory needs to be assessed in practice, to see whether diversifying assets really does offer a superior return for a given level of risk, and a lower level of risk for a given return.

3.2 Portfolio Diversification

Consider a two asset portfolio once again, with proportion P1 invested in asset 1 and proportion P2 invested in asset 2. As noted earlier the variance of an asset is its standard deviation squared, SD^2. This means the variance of asset 1 is $SD1^2$, and the variance of asset 2 equals $SD2^2$. The variance of the two asset portfolio, SDp^2, would be:

$$SDp^2 = P1^2*SD1^2 + P2^2*SD2^2 + 2*P1*P2*cov(P1, P2)$$

The standard deviation would be the positive square root of the variance, while the term cov(P1, P2) refers to the covariance between proportion 1 (of asset 1), and proportion 2 (of asset 2).

Most of the portfolio variance formula here is self-explanatory, as individual standard deviation values are weighted by their proportion in the portfolio, but there are two things which require further explanation. While the first two parts of the equation referring to individual variance are squared the third and final part for covariance isn't, and this is because covariance focuses on the rate of change between variables. Differentiation is required to find this change and performing this on the third part of the formula replaces the 'squared' with a 'multiplied by two' instead, as differentiation multiplies the power of a variable by its coefficient and then reduces the power by one. The other part of the equation that needs developing is the cov(P1, P2) piece, and this needs to be replaced with something that can be calculated:

$$cov(P1, P2) = E\ (P1 - E(P1))(P2 - E(P2))$$

This is the same formula as used for variance above, except that the return (R) is replaced by the proportion made up from each asset (P1 and P2). To find the correlation coefficient showing the relationship between asset 1 and asset 2, C12 for short, we simply take this 'covariance' and remove the 'variance' to leave only the 'co' part, which is short for correlation. To remove the variance we would normally divide by SD^2, but as the formula here includes two assets we divide by SD1*SD2 instead:

$$C12 = cov(P1, P2)\ /\ SD1*SD2$$

If we already had the correlation coefficient between the two assets, C12, then this equation could be rearranged to make cov(P1, P2) the subject:

$$cov(P1, P2) = C12*SD1*SD2$$

This can be put back into the formula for the overall portfolio variance above:

$$SDp^2 = P1^2*SD1^2 + P2^2*SD2^2 + 2*P1*P2*C12*SD1*SD2$$

With this completed formula some conclusions can be made about portfolio variance. It's determined by the proportion of wealth made up from each asset, the standard deviation (i.e. risk) of each asset, and the correlation coefficient (C12) between the two assets. As a result, if there was no correlation between the assets, C12 = 0, then portfolio variance depends only on the sum of individual asset variances:

$$SDp^2 = P1^2*SD1^2 + P2^2*SD2^2$$

If the two assets were complements with identical behaviour to external factors there would be no reduction in risk from holding both, and this perfect positive correlation between the assets, C12 = 1, would see increased portfolio variance with an additional term compared to the previous example:

$$SDp^2 = P1^2*SD1^2 + P2^2*SD2^2 + 2*P1*P2*C12*SD1*SD2$$

And if the two assets were exact opposites there would be the maximum possible reduction in risk from holding both assets, and this perfect negative correlation between the assets, C12 = -1, would see the lowest possible portfolio variance. Not only would here not be an additional term added to the sum of individual variances, but instead this term would be subtracted from the portfolio variance:

$$SDp^2 = P1^2*SD1^2 + P2^2*SD2^2 - 2*P1*P2*C12*SD1*SD2$$

This shows that the further the correlation between assets moves away from +1 and perfect positive correlation, such as with two identical assets, the lower the portfolio variance (i.e. risk) will be. This supports the idea that diversification of investments will reduce risk.

For example, there may be two assets making up a portfolio where each asset has the following characteristics:

Asset 1: E(R1) = 25%, SD1 = 8%;
Asset 2: E(R2) = 18%, SD2 = 4%.

The expected return of the portfolio would depend on the proportion invested in each asset, and if it was 50% of each then the expected portfolio return may be calculated:

$$E(Rp) = P1*E(R1) + P2*E(R2)$$
$$E(Rp) = 0.5*0.25 + 0.5*0.18 = 21.5\%$$

The portfolio risk, SDp, will depend on the correlation coefficient between the two assets, C12, and the proportion that each asset plays in the portfolio. The diagram below shows the various possible levels of portfolio risk, depending on the correlation coefficient (C12) between the two assets in the portfolio.

If the two assets are perfectly correlated to external factors with C12 = 1 (i.e. complements), then the line AB represents portfolio risk. Point A shows the expected return and risk associated with asset 1, with a 25% return and 8% standard deviation (SD), while point B shows the expected return and risk associated with asset 2, with an 18% return and 4% SD. As the proportion invested in each asset changes an investor moves along the line AB, and more invested in asset A sees a move toward that point etc.

Portfolio diversification

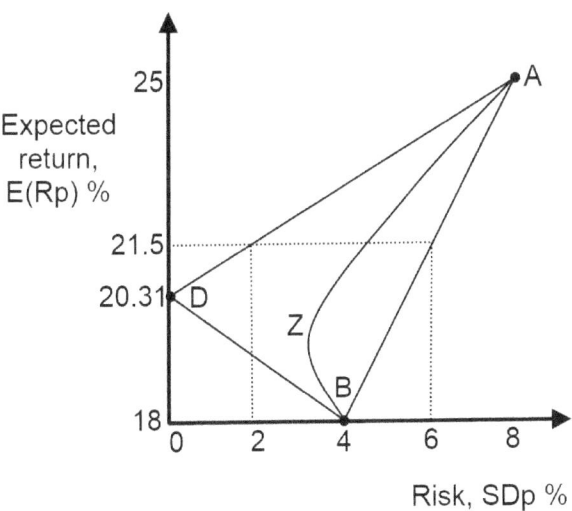

If there is instead perfect negative correlation between the two assets in the portfolio, C12 = -1, then shape ADB represents portfolio risk. The D stands for diversified, as the new shape represents the effects of portfolio diversification with stocks that will react in different ways to market changes. Point A represents asset 1 as before, and point B represents asset 2, while the new point D represents how the two could be combined in optimal amounts to get a high return with no risk whatsoever.

Asset 1 and asset 2 are perfectly negatively correlated in this scenario, and that means that if asset 1 rises by 10% asset 2 will fall by 10%, and if asset 1 falls by 5% then asset two will rise by 5%, etc. This allows for 'hedging' to take place, where an investment can be positioned to offset potential portfolio gains or losses from another investment.

Asset 1 has a 25% expected return and 8% SD risk, while asset 2 has an 18% expected return and 4% SD risk, but if asset 2 made up twice the proportion in the portfolio as asset 1 then the two sources of risk could be balanced out. Two sets of asset 2 gives a 36% return (18%*2) overall and an 8% risk exposure level (4%*2), the same risk as asset 1. This will ensure no risk at all, as if the stock of asset 1 rose/fell with an 8% sensitivity to the market asset 2's presence in the portfolio would fall/rise with an 8% sensitivity in the opposite direction.

In order for asset 1 and asset 2 to be perfectly balanced, with asset 2 making up twice the amount in the portfolio as asset 1 to hedge against any possible loss, asset 1 would have to make up a third of the portfolio (33.33%) and asset 2 the remaining two thirds (66.67%). We already know that this would give risk of 0%, but the expected portfolio return needs to be calculated too:

$$E(Rp) = P1*E(R1) + P2*E(R2)$$
$$E(Rp) = 0.33*0.25 + 0.67*0.18$$
$$E(Rp) = 0.0825 + 0.1206$$
$$E(Rp) = 20.31 \text{ or } 20.31\%$$

The point labelled D in the image shows the 20.31% expected return and 0% SD risk.

Finally, shape AZB in the image shows the situation where there is zero correlation between the two assets in the portfolio, $C12 = 0$. As the image suggests, this gives less risk than perfect positive correlation where $C12 = 1$, and more risk than perfect negative correlation where $C12 = -1$. Zero correlation is halfway between the two extremes of perfect positive or negative correlation, and shape AZB is halfway between line AB and shape ADB as a result.

The dotted lines in the image show that portfolio diversification can reduce risk for a given expected return. If assets are perfectly positively correlated, then line AB gives portfolio risk and an expected return of 21.5 % is associated with SD risk of 6%. But in a fully diversified portfolio with assets perfectly negatively correlated, shape

ADB represents the portfolio risk and the expected return of 21.5% is associated with SD risk of roughly 2%. This is a huge decrease in risk without lessening the return.

Just as diversification reduces risk in a two asset portfolio it will also reduce risk with a greater number of assets. The diagram below shows the possible effects of portfolio diversification with multiple assets.

3 asset diversified portfolio

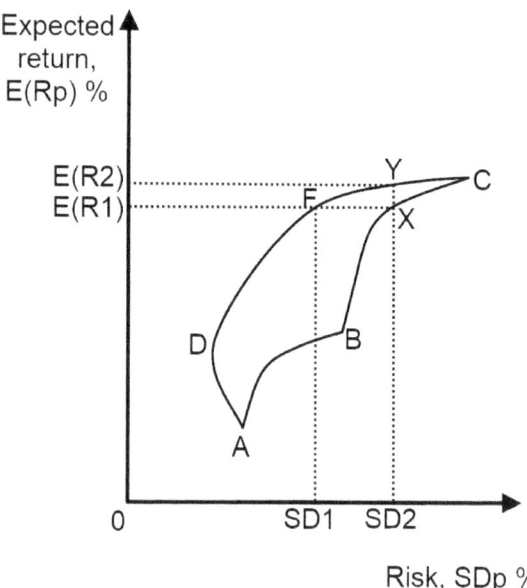

This diagram is for a three asset portfolio, where points A, B and C represent the expected return and corresponding risk for three individual assets. Asset A has low risk and low expected return, asset B has higher values for both factors, while asset C has the highest expected return but also the highest risk of the three assets in the portfolio. The shape CBA, that starts at point C goes through point B and ends at point A, represents some degree of positive correlation between the three assets.

Alternatively, the shape CFD, starting at point C and passing though point F before ending at point D, represents a scenario where there is instead extensive diversification in the portfolio and negative correlation between the three assets. Point A transforms to point D, with a higher expected return and lower risk, while the same happens as point B transforms into point F. The result of diversification is a more efficient portfolio, with efficient frontier CFD far better than frontier CBA.

The superiority of the diversified three asset portfolio is shown by points F, X, and Y. Without diversification the investor was stuck on the CBA curve at a point such as X, with the corresponding levels of expected return and standard deviation. But with diversification into negatively correlated assets he moves to curve CFD, and points Y and F are then available. Point Y has the same risk as point X had, at level SD2, but its expected return is higher at E(R2) instead of E(R1). And point F has the same return as point X, at E(R1), but the risk is lower at SD1 in place of SD2.

Indifference curve analysis can be added, as higher curves and utility depend on lower risk and higher returns.

With little or no portfolio diversification the shape CBA gives the possible expected return and risk resulting from holding the three assets. The best available outcome for an investor is to be on indifference curve I1, at point B. But with a greater level of portfolio diversification the curve CFD is available, with a greater expected return and lower risk. Now a far higher indifference curve, I3, is available at point X, and the investor can reach it by adjusting the proportions each of the three assets take up in the portfolio, to move along curve CFD.

Utility gains from diversification

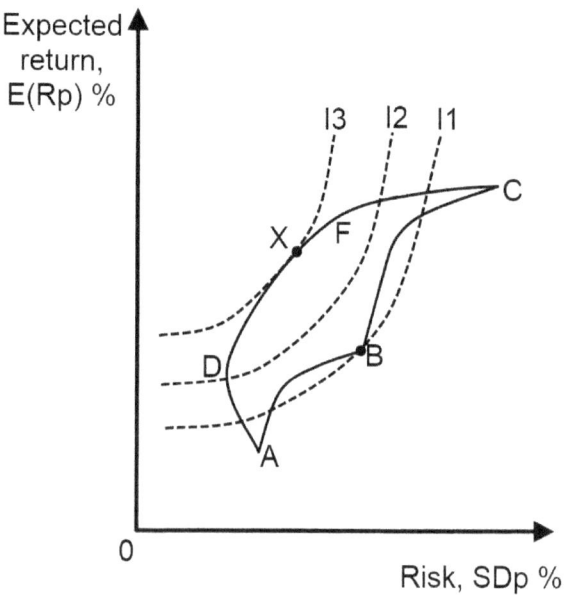

The benefits of portfolio diversification holds with a range of investor preferences, such as greater levels of risk aversion or risk seeking. The next diagram shows the same indifference curve I3 as before which the investor can achieve at point X. But two additional curves are added, one for a more risk adverse investor whose highest indifference curve meets shape CFD at point RA (risk averse), and one for a more risk seeking investor whose highest indifference curve meets shape CFD at point RS (risk seeking).

Risk aversion and risk seeking

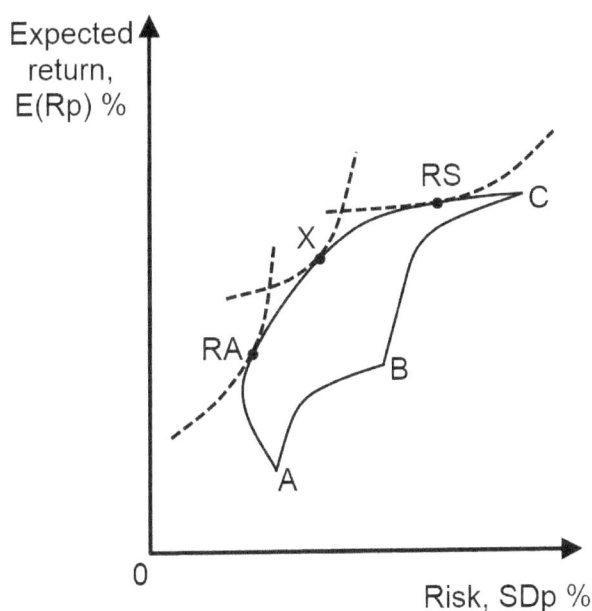

While the original investor at equilibrium point X reaches a higher indifference curve and gains higher utility by moving up left in the diagram, increasing returns and lowering risk in roughly equal amounts, the more risk averse and risk seeking investors have difference preferences. The risk averse investor gains utility by more leftward movements that lower risk, and increasing the expected return is less of a focus, while the risk seeking investor gains from more upward movements that increase the return, and reducing the risk is not as important to him. As the diagram suggests the diversified portfolio curve CFD allows all of these, and is better for all types of investors compared to original curve CBA. They can all each reach a higher indifference curve by adjusting the proportions the three negatively correlated assets make up in their portfolio.

3.3 A Risk-Free Asset

Portfolio diversification can reduce risk without sacrificing the return, but to reach the equilibrium point where an investor is on the highest possible indifference curve involves a great deal of work. It requires information on the exact correlations between assets to allow efficient asset selection for a portfolio, and then the chosen assets must be selected in the right proportions or the equilibrium point will be missed. This process simply isn't feasible for the average investor, and a more simple way of reaching the equilibrium return and risk is required.

Introducing a risk-free asset can help reach the equilibrium without requiring extensive information about individual assets. An example of a risk-free asset would be a government bond, as this isn't vulnerable to market ups and downs, and is secured by the protection of the government. The risk-free asset (Rf) has guaranteed levels of expected return, E(Rf), and standard deviation, SDf:

$$E(Rf) = Rf$$
$$SDf = 0$$

In a two asset portfolio made up with a proportion (Pf) of a risk-free asset (Rf) and a proportion (Pa) of a risky asset (Ra), Caf represents the correlation between the risky and risk-free asset, while E(Ra) and E(Rf) give the corresponding expected returns, and SDa and SDf the respective standard deviations. The expected return of the portfolio, E(Rp), and its variance risk, SDp^2, are below:

$$E(Rp) = Pa*E(Ra) + Pf*E(Rf) = Pa*E(Ra) + Pf*Rf$$
$$SDp^2 = Pa^2*SDa^2 + Pf^2*SDf^2 - 2*Pa*Pf*Caf*SDa*SDf$$

The expected return follows the same formula as before, but because $SDf = 0$ the portfolio variance SDp^2 and portfolio standard deviation SDp can be simplified:

$$SDp^2 = Pa^2*SDa^2$$
$$SDp = Pa*SDa$$

Portfolio risk will only depend on the standard deviation of the risky asset, as the risk-free asset comes with no risk. With the return and risk levels for both risk-free and risky assets an efficient boundary can be drawn for the portfolio, and this is simply a line connecting both points on the familiar return against risk graph.

Rf on the diagram represents the risk-free, with expected return (and actual return, as there's no risk) at the level shown. Ra represents the risky asset, with risk at level SDa, and an expected return of E(Ra), a higher return than that of the risk-free asset to reward taking on more risk.

A risk-free asset

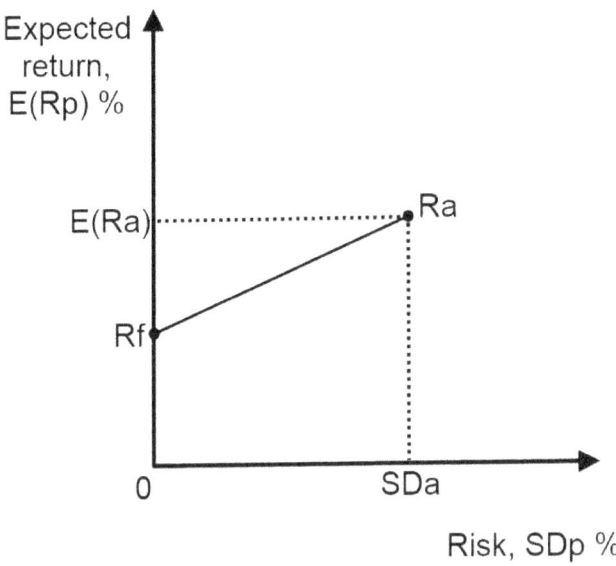

The slope of the line in the image gives the incremental expected return for an additional unit of risk, which can be denoted as $\Delta E(R)$. It can be found with the following formula:

$$\Delta E(R) = (E(Ra) - Rf) / SDa$$

A risk-free asset can also be combined with an entire risky portfolio, such as the diversified three asset portfolio looked at earlier.

Risk-free asset and diversified portfolio

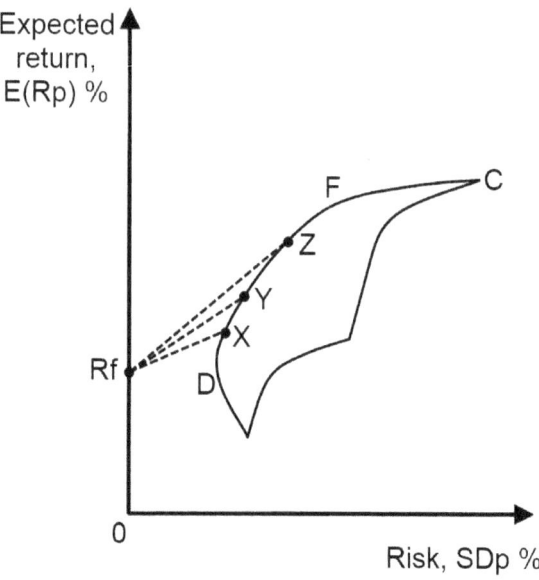

Remember that the three asset portfolio, diversified with negatively correlated assets, gave an efficient frontier of shape CFD. And the risk-free rate can be combined with any point on this frontier for an efficient portfolio. Point X offers a higher overall portfolio return if a little risk is taken on, point Y offers a greater return but comes with more risk, while point Z continues this trend, and so on. A range of risk-return boundaries are available to suit an investor's risk tolerance level.

There may also be a situation where an investor would be prepared to take on higher risk for a higher return, but lacks the funds to acquire the required assets. In this case the investor could borrow returns at the risk-return rate for borrowing. Alternatively, there may be an investor whose accumulated assets give him a higher return than he needs, and he may be willing to lend out some of his returns at the risk-return rate for lending. The diagram below shows both scenarios, assuming different rates for borrowing and lending, again using the well diversified three asset portfolio combined with the risk-free rate.

Borrowing and lending rates

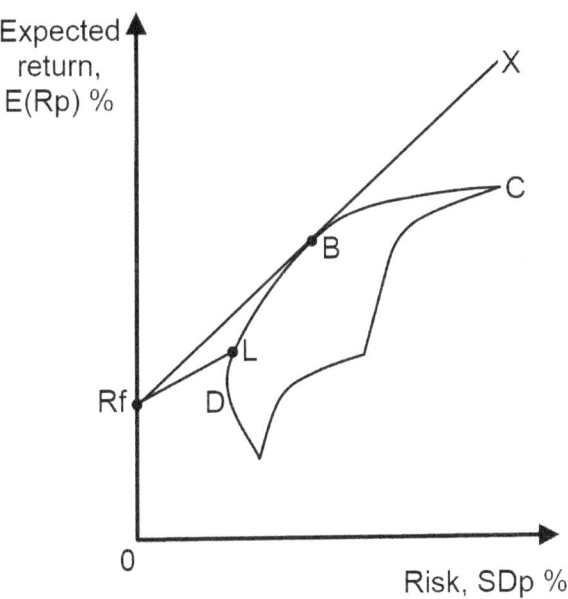

The line from Rf through point B to point X represents the rate for borrowing, and the line from Rf to point L represents the rate for lending. An investor could borrow at the borrowing rate all the way up to point X, and achieve a higher return than he had available before, although this comes with greater risk. Alternatively, a lender who had a higher return than he required could lend out at the (worse) risk-return rate for lending, loaning out anywhere from point L if he kept all his investments, or all the way to point Rf if he loaned out everything except the freely available risk-free rate.

Individual indifference curves will decide which point a lender or borrower selects, but it will be somewhere on the Rf to L line for a lender, or on the Rf to X line for a borrower. The borrowing and lending rates here transform the set of efficient points, and the curve from C to D is replaced by a far narrower efficient frontier starting at point B and ending at L. Points between D and L or between B and C now offer a comparatively lower return for the same level of risk, and shouldn't be selected.

In the previous diagram there is a small efficient frontier, determined by the difference between the rate for borrowing and the rate for lending. But if the borrowing and lending rates were identical then there would be only a single equilibrium point. The next section looks into this scenario and the resulting effects on portfolio selection.

3.4 Market Portfolio and Capital Market Line

In an efficient market there's only one rate of interest, and the risk-free rate (Rf) is the same as the rate for borrowing (Rb) and the rate for lending (Rl):

$$Rf = Rb = Rl$$

With only one rate of interest the efficient boundary becomes a straight line between the risk-free rate and the portfolio efficient frontier, and this is known as the capital market line (CML). All investors will hold only one portfolio, the market portfolio (M), with expected return E(RM) and standard deviation risk of SDM. They will then lend or borrow according to their individual preferences, and those who lend will invest instead in the risk-free asset offering a risk-free rate. The capital market line and market portfolio is shown in the diagram, where the CML slope equals the market return minus the risk-free rate, divided by the market risk: (E(RM) - Rf) / SDM.

The equation for the CML gives an efficient portfolio's expected return, E(Reff), where SDeff is an efficient portfolio's risk, and Z is the market price of risk (risk premium) given by the CML slope:

$$E(R_{eff}) = R_f + [(E(R_M) - R_f) / SD_M] * SD_{eff}$$
$$E(R_{eff}) = R_f + Z * SD_{eff}$$

Market portfolio and capital market line

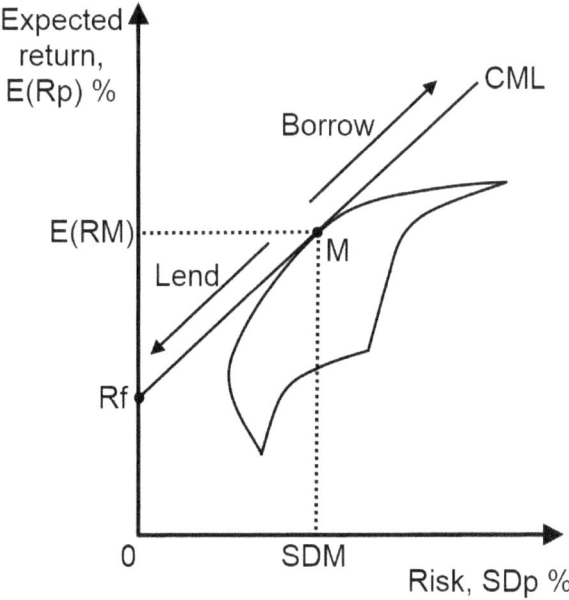

This selection of this market portfolio irrespective of risk attitude and tolerance allows a separation of risk-return preferences and investment, and is known as the Tobin Separation Theorem (Tobin, 1958), similar to the Fisher Separation Theorem examined earlier.

The result that all investors will buy the market portfolio and then buy or lend as their preferences suggest is a powerful one, but it depends on the following assumptions:

1) Investors seek to maximize their utility from wealth;

2) Choices depend only on expected return and risk;

3) Unlimited borrowing and lending at risk-free rate;

4) Perfect markets, with no taxes or transaction costs;

5) Perfect information is available to all investors;

6) Decision-making time horizon equal for all investors.

In reality some of these assumptions may not hold, but they offer a useful starting point into understanding how investors will behave, and why they will all select only the market portfolio. The market index comprises shares of all companies and therefore contains all risky assets, and is also considered the most reliable representation of equilibrium prices, where the expected return corresponds to the associated risk, as by containing so many assets any individual mistake in asset pricing should be aggregated away. By containing all possible assets the market portfolio provides maximum diversification, which will lower risk up to a point for the reasons explained above, as negatively correlated assets can counteract possible losses in certain circumstances with equivalent gains.

4 Capital Asset Pricing Model (CAPM)

4.1 Systematic Risk

The risk reduction associated with portfolio diversification only holds to a certain point, and the non-diversifiable or systemic risk inherent to all firms can't be diversified away.

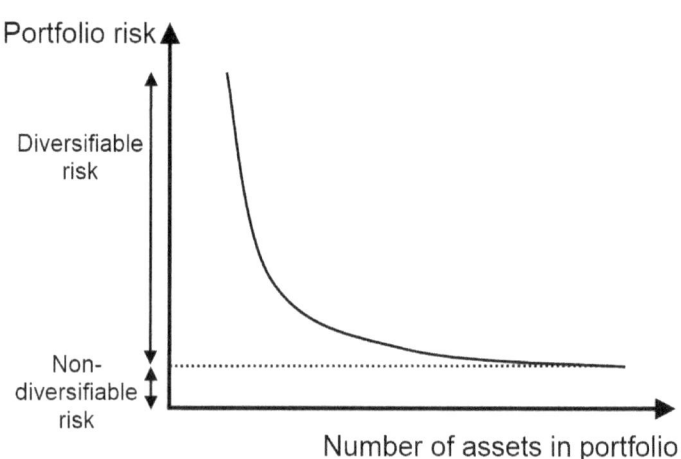

While diversifiable risk refers to the variability of returns due to unique or specific factors that affect the individual firm, systematic or non-diversifiable risk relates to the risk arising from non-specific or market factors affecting all assets that are traded. For a well diversified portfolio such as the market portfolio only the market risk matters, which shows how sensitive an asset is to movements in the market. There is no gain to an investor for taking on diversifiable risk, and an efficient portfolio will avoid it by containing the market portfolio as shown in the last section. Individual investors are only rewarded for taking on systematic risk, and stocks and securities will have different amounts of systematic risk associated with them.

Systematic risk can have a significant impact on asset prices and can affect the variability of share price returns, while the market factors also determine the cash flow of the firm, and with it share price movements and dividend levels. The main determinants of a firm's systematic risk exposure are the sensitivity of a firm's revenues to the general level of economic activity, the degree of cost sensitivity, and the level of leverage/gearing (i.e. the amount of debt, whether from borrowing money, accumulating fixed assets, or using derivatives).

4.2 CAPM Assumptions and Expression

While selection of the market portfolio reduces diversifiable risk, another strategy is required to deal with unavoidable systematic risk. As this risk can't be reduced all an investor can do is target assets with the best return relative to the given risk level. To undertake this analysis requires an asset pricing model, and that is the focus of this section.

The capital asset pricing model (CAPM) is considered to be the foremost model of its kind for investors, and it prices assets based upon their systematic risk. The model has some simplifying assumptions, several of which have already been seen before in a similar form:

1) Investors and risk averse and aim to maximize expected utility and achieve the highest possible indifference curve;

2) Investors are price takers with no influence over price levels, and they have the same expectations;

3) All investors can lend or borrow at the same risk-free rate;

4) The total quantity of assets is fixed and all assets are perfectly divisible;

5) Perfect and costless information is available to all investors;

6) There are perfect capital markets, with no taxes, transaction or regulation costs.

An individual asset's (i) relationship between risk and expected return depends upon the following factors: the individual asset's expected return, $E(R_i)$; risk-free rate, R_f; expected return of the market portfolio, $E(R_M)$; covariance between the returns on the individual asset and those of the market, $cov(i, M)$; and the variance on market returns, SDM^2. The relationship is given below:

$$E(R_i) = R_f + (E(R_M) - R_f)*[cov(i, M) / SDM^2]$$

In the CAPM expression only one element refers directly to the individual asset (i), and that's its covariance with the market return, $cov(i, M)$. All other parts of the expression relate to factors common to all assets. Therefore the factor that determines an asset's expected return is the extent to which the expected returns of the asset vary with those of the market portfolio. The $cov(i, M)$ term represents the systematic risk of the individual firm, but it is inseparable from market risk. As the expected return expression above shows, the return for an asset is not determined by any risk that is specific to it, but only the risks coming from the market. The higher the value of $cov(i, M)$, the greater the level of systematic risk associated with a particular asset and the higher its expected return should be.

The final term in the CAPM expression, cov(i, M) / SDM^2, is usually referred to as beta, (ß), and therefore:

$$ßi = cov(i, M) / SDM^2$$

As a result the CAPM is usually referred to as follows:

$$E(Ri) = Rf + (E(RM) - Rf)*ßi$$

4.3 Security Market Line and Asset Valuation

With known beta and expected return values an efficient frontier can once again be created for assets, and as seen earlier this starts at the risk-free rate and passes through the market portfolio. In portfolio theory this frontier plots the expected return against the standard deviation (SD) risk of an individual asset or portfolio, and is called the capital market line (CML), but here the SD risk is replaced with beta risk and the CML is replaced with the security market line (SML). The capital market line showed the most efficient way to achieve capital, using maximum portfolio diversification with the risk-free rate and market portfolio for a superior risk-return rate. But the security market line shows an asset's level of security in the face of market change, and the line from the risk-free rate the through the market portfolio shows total covariance with the market, to allow a comparative assessment of other assets.

The diagram shows the risk-free rate, Rf, market portfolio, M, and two other assets, A and B. While the Rf has a beta of 0 (risk-free means no risk of any type), the market portfolio has a beta value of 1, while A and B have beta values of 0.6 and 1.4 respectively.

Security market line

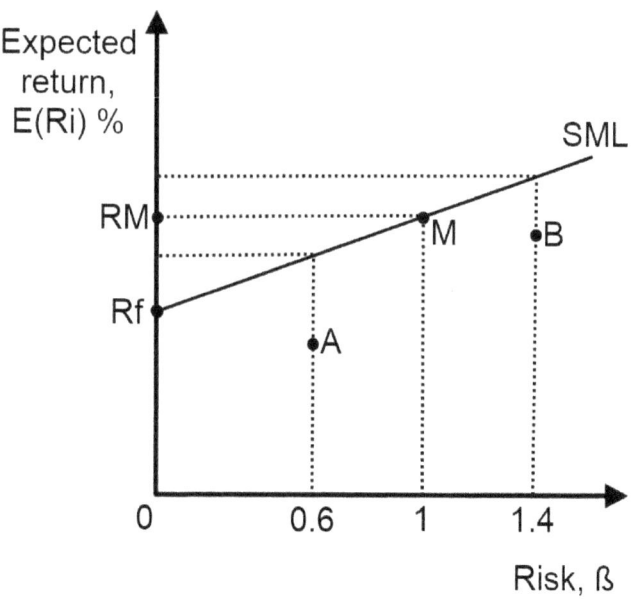

The beta value for an asset represents the responsiveness of its expected return relative to movements in the market's expected return:

ß > 1 means E(Ri) will be expected to rise or fall by more than the % change in the market (i.e. asset return is more sensitive than the market);

ß < 1 means E(Ri) will be expected to rise or fall by less than the % change in the market (i.e. asset return is less sensitive than the market);

ß = 1 means E(Ri) will be expected to rise or fall by the same % change in the market (i.e. asset return is equally as sensitive as the market).

As the market return will naturally rise or fall by the same % change as the market (because it is the market), the market portfolio M has a beta value of 1 as shown above. Asset B in the graph has a beta value of 1.4 as noted, and whatever happens to the market will see an exaggerated reaction in asset B's expected return. The SML shows the return that should be associated with this level of risk, based on the market risk premium, and its own risk-return rate relative to the risk-free rate. According to the graph a beta of 1.4 should come with an expected return above the market return, but here the return is actually lower than the market's and asset B is therefore overpriced in relative terms, with too low a return for its level of risk. Its stock price is too high, which pulls down the expected return for those who invest in it, and asset B looks to be one to avoid.

Asset A in the graph has a beta of 0.6, and the events in the market are met by an underweighted response in the return of asset A. This means there's less risk associated with this security than with the market portfolio, and as a result a lower return would be acceptable. The SML again shows the expected return that should be associated with a 0.6 level of beta risk, and it should be somewhere above the risk-free rate but below the market return. However, the graph shows that asset A's expected return is even lower than the risk-free rate, and any investor in this asset would take on risk for nothing, as the freely available risk-free rate offers a higher return. Asset A is overpriced just like asset B and again it should be avoided, as it isn't worth the opportunity cost of sacrificing additional investment in the risk-free rate and market portfolio.

Beta is essentially a discount factor, showing how an asset's expected return needs to be adjusted to offer the same risk-return rate as the risk-free rate and market portfolio on the safe security market line. But it doesn't say anything about the volatility of individual asset returns, and that is only given by standard deviation and the capital market line. The capital asset pricing model (CAPM) uses an asset's beta level to determine whether an asset sits on the security market line (SML), below the line, or above it. If an asset is below the line then it's overpriced, and if it's above the line then it's underpriced.

Investors use the CAPM to decide which assets are worth their investment, while finance managers may use it to derive discount rates to calculate and manage costs for their investment projects. Applying the CAPM takes freely available information to first determine expected return or risk values in the situation where assets sit on the SML. Once it's known what the return and risk values should be this can be compared to information on what they actually are, and the choice of investment projects can take place.

Asset evaluation

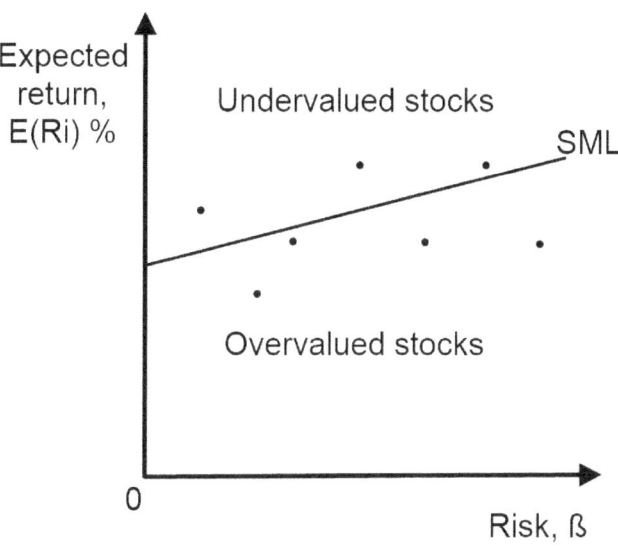

Investors use the CAPM to decide which assets are worth their investment, while finance managers may use it to derive discount rates to calculate and manage costs for their investment projects. Using the CAPM takes available information to determine expected return or risk values in the situation where assets sit on the SML. Once it's known what the return and risk values should be based upon the SML, this can compared to information on what they really are and the choice of investments can then take place. Those with a better return than the SML for a given risk level, or lower risk for a given return will be preferred.

For example, suppose an asset (i) has a covariance with the market of 0.042 or 4.2%, while the standard deviation of returns on the representative market portfolio is 0.25, or 25%. The beta, ß, of the asset can be found with only these two pieces of information, to show how the asset under consideration would respond to changes in the market if it sat on the SML:

$$ß_i = cov(i, M) / SDM^2$$
$$ß_i = 0.042 / 0.25^2$$
$$ß_i = 0.672$$

This asset has a beta of 0.672 if it sits on the SML, and as the market changes this asset's returns will increase or fall at a reduced scale of 0.672, or roughly two thirds. This information can then be used by investors to prepare their cost schedules, and if financial experts predicted that the market's returns could fall by up to 10% in the near future, then the investor would know that the returns from asset (i) could fall by up to 6.72%. It would therefore be wise for them not to count on a fixed future income above this level when taking on costs for an investment project.

Once the investor has the beta value he needs to fill in the rest of the CAPM expression, to find the expected return of the asset under consideration:

$$E(R_i) = R_f + (E(R_M) - R_f)*ß_i$$

The expected return on the market could be found by looking at financial sources, and the predicated rate of return might be 4% as an example. A risk-free rate will also be available using government bills and that is at 2% here. With this information the expected return of the asset can be calculated in the case where it lay on the security market line:

$$E(R_i) = 0.02 + (0.04 - 0.02)*0.672$$
$$E(R_i) = 0.02 + 0.01344$$
$$E(R_i) = 0.03344 \text{ or } 3.344\%$$

This asset's SML expected return is 3.34%, higher than the risk-free rate of 2% to suggest it could be a worthwhile investment, but lower than the market return of 4% to cause some doubts. But if the investor only required a return of 3% to meet his income needs, and would prefer to avoid the more erratic movements in returns that come with the market in this case (up to a 10% fall as noted), he may prefer the less sensitive asset (i). Perhaps significant and frequent changes in returns will cause higher 'menu costs' where nominal prices must be constantly changed, and may see his customers grow annoyed and lose faith in the business, to cause a downturn in demand and profit as a result. If this were the case then asset (i) may be more appealing than the market portfolio and chosen over it in the investment decision.

The CAPM can also be used in a different way, and instead of finding the expected return using the beta value, the pricing model can use the known return to find the beta.

For example, if another asset (k) was thought to deliver an expected return of 7.5% the CAPM expression would be used in reverse:

$$E(R_k) = R_f + (E(R_M) - R_f) * \beta_k$$
$$0.075 = 0.02 + (0.04 - 0.02) * \beta_k$$
$$0.055 = (0.02) * \beta_k$$
$$\beta_k = 0.055 / 0.02$$
$$\beta_k = 2.75$$

This asset would have a beta of 2.75 if it sat on the SML. In a stable market environment where the market return was not expected to change much this asset (k) may be best, as it offers a 7.5% return which is far higher than the market rate. Although any rise or fall in the market would see the asset's returns follow the same pattern, only multiplied by a factor of 2.75, if the market was in a steady state with little if any changes expected then this may never come into play.

But before the investor decides whether to purchase asset (i), asset (k), or neither, based on the position he seeks on the security market line, he should first use any other available information to determine whether they sit below or above the SML. This will tell him if they are overvalued or undervalued respectively.

For example, perhaps the firm to which asset (i) relates has recently released a financial report, and this predicts that the firm is on course for only a 2.5% expected return, lower than previously thought, following an unexpected significant problem with one of their supply chains. In this scenario the expected return would put the asset below the SML, as a beta of 0.672 should be associated with a higher expected return of 3.34%, and this means asset (i) is overvalued and not worth investment.

It's also possible that the beta value calculated for asset (k) is incorrect. An investor may make their own estimation of beta, ß, using statistical software to regress asset (k)'s monthly returns (capital gains plus dividends as a fraction of share price), against returns on the market portfolio. The result may suggest that the real beta value is 2.8, higher than the previously assumed beta of 2.75 but associated with only a 7.5% expected return. This greater risk would put asset (k) to the right of the SML and therefore below it, to suggest asset (k) is also overvalued and to be avoided.

But just as the data evidence can suggest that assets are overvalued, inefficient, and to be avoided, the same may also be true for the CAPM model itself. If the estimated expected return or estimated beta are different from what the CAPM would predict then this suggests the model is flawed. It's possible to test the CAPM directly with a regression, using historical values of an asset's returns for a time period, Ri_t, the risk-free rate for a time period, Rf_t, and the beta of an asset, $ß_i$. The relevant regressions equation is below.

$$Ri_t - Rf_t = \alpha + b*ßi + \varepsilon i_t$$

The equation says that the excess return for asset (i) for a time period (the return on the asset minus the risk-free rate), equals a constant factor, α (known as 'alpha'), and the asset's beta multiplied by an unknown coefficient, and a random error factor, ε, known as epsilon. If the CAPM model is accurate then the expected (excess) return should only depend on beta, as shown by the diagrams earlier. The regression should show factor b to be the only significant explanatory variable to suggest that beta is important, while α, showing the presence of another constant factor, and ε, showing a one-off random factor, should be statistically insignificant and therefore have no influence over the expected (excess) return an asset offers.

Statistical significance of one-off error as given by ε would ask some questions of the robustness of the CAPM, and if a constant factor α was both significant and positive it would challenge the use of the whole model, as it suggests that stocks have a constant excess return and are therefore undervalued. The CAPM predicts that assets will lie on the line or below it, making the market portfolio the equilibrium choice, but if assets are undervalued that would push investors away from the market portfolio into profit-seeking with individual assets, destroying the whole idea of an efficient market portfolio, the capital market line, and the security market line. The next section looks into the empirical evidence on beta and the CAPM to see whether they hold up in practice.

4.4 Empirical Evidence on the CAPM

First the evidence against the CAPM will be put forward, and Fama and MacBeth (1973) are among those who estimate that the constant factor alpha, α, is positive, and higher than the risk-free rate of return. The beta coefficient, b, was found to be flatter than theory predicts, while empirical analysis indicated that other variables are significant in explaining expected returns.

Fama and French (1992) studied US stocks over 1962-89 and found that the beta value does not account for asset returns, while small companies and those with a high book value (high ratio of balance sheet to market value of equity) had returns greater than the CAPM would suggest, and were undervalued. Others have found similar results on the influence of these factors, and Davis, Fama, and French (2000) added size and book-to-market risk premium factors to the CAPM. They test the model for the period 1929-97 and find it a superior predictor of returns than the original one factor beta model.

But Chan and Lakonishok (1993) argue that the one factor beta model should not be discarded entirely, as the relationship between beta and expected returns varies over time. Black (1993) claims that Fama and French's results are unreliable as they had to 'data mine' to achieve their results, i.e. they looked for evidence that supports the conclusion they already had in mind, and ignored everything that supported the original CAPM. Kandel and Stambaugh (1995) agree with this idea as do Kothari, Shanken and Sloan (1995). They find that beta works in a single factor model if annual returns are used, as opposed to dividing returns into shorter periods, and if the regression uses the GLS (generalized least squares) method instead of the OLS (ordinary least squares) method. The OLS method assumes perfect efficiency, while the GLS method that supports beta and the CAPM allows for a little inefficiency, with non-constant standard deviation and some correlation in observations.

Hsia, Fuller and Chen (2000) offer an explanation for the evidence against and for the beta based CAPM. They find that capital market frictions are an important factor in determining its explanatory power. If market frictions are not substantial then beta should be 'alive' as a powerful explanatory factor, as used in the CAPM. But with important market frictions other factors will be needed to complement beta. This may explain why Fama and French (1992) found evidence against beta and the CAPM using monthly returns, but Kothari, Shanken and Sloan (1995) found evidence for it with annual returns. The shorter monthly period is more likely to emphasize natural market frictions, while the longer yearly returns should see this aggregated away.

Hsia, Fuller and Chen (2000) adopt a 'moving average beta' approach in place of the usual method of using a fixed value for a period, and the beta is calculated on lead and lag data and moves with it over time. They find that this moving average beta is very much alive, and can predict expected returns as the CAPM suggests. Ang and Chen (2007) find that a conditional CAPM based on time-varying betas can work, and with a predictable market risk premium over the risk-free rate (i.e. low market frictions), they find that the alpha, α, for a book-to-market factor, one of the alternative explanatory factors put forward by CAPM critics, is statistically insignificant.

Roll (1977) argues that the CAPM is simply untestable and we can never know whether it's a good model or not, and therefore it may be a mistake to rely on it. This is based on the fact that the CAPM uses a market portfolio, but in reality it's impossible to identify such as thing as it would have to include all assets including things such as human capital and consumer durables, which are very difficult to value, and the market index is a poor proxy. Ross (1976) also doubts the market equilibrium based CAPM, and comes up with an alternative arbitrage pricing theory multi-factor model, including variables based on macroeconomic factors in place of a single market equilibrium portfolio.

Overall it seems that the validity of the CAPM model depends upon the level of market frictions and the market portfolio equilibrium. In simple terms, any test of the CAPM model is really a joint hypothesis test of market efficiency, and in turn any test of market efficiency depends upon the validity of the model used to price assets. With this in mind the next step has to be to examine the issue of market efficiency, and the next chapter addresses this in depth.

5 Market Efficiency

5.1 Efficient Market Hypothesis

Earlier chapters have looked into how investors may take on risk to attain higher returns, using an asset pricing model such as the CAPM to determine the stocks to select. But all of this is based on the idea that capital markets are efficient, even 'perfect', and that market prices reflect all available information, and there's no way to use the available information to make excess profits, whether you're an individual investor or a firm. An efficient market may be defined by operational efficiency, allocational efficiency, and price efficiency. It should encourage the purchase of shares, ensure an efficient allocation of resources, and provide the correct signals to finance managers. All of these depend on the market accurately representing all available information.

If market prices are not efficient then they give misleading information of the intrinsic value of assets/securities, and no asset pricing model will be accurate and nor will the market itself. A market or asset pricing model that doesn't function properly is essentially useless and non-existent, and all of the benefits that these offer, such as Fisher separation theorem where ownership and financing can be separated from investment, or using portfolio theory to reduce risk through diversification of assets, will be impossible. Investors must know whether or not the market is efficient to adjust their behaviour accordingly.

Kendall (1953) originated the idea that the price of securities follow a 'random walk' that can't be predicted, as they reflect all new information which will naturally be random. This implies efficiency as people can't rip others off with prices that are too high, or make excess profits buying assets when prices are too low, if they can't predict what the prices will be in the future.

Eugene Fama (1965) argued that competition by many market participants creates a situation where, at any point in time, the actual prices of securities reflect both the effects of information relating to events that have already occurred, and also those which may be expected by the market to occur in the future. In other words, in an efficient market the actual price of a security at any time will give a good estimate of its intrinsic value. This is made possible by two separate factors. First the quality of the price adjustment, which should incorporate all new information to ensure security prices change to the full extent that current or expected value changes, and firms can't fool investors into paying more for stocks than they're worth. The second factor is the speed of this adjustment, as market prices change before investors can use the newly available information to buy/sell and make excess returns.

Fama's theory that the market is efficient is known as the efficient market hypothesis (EMH). The idea is shown in visual form in the image below.

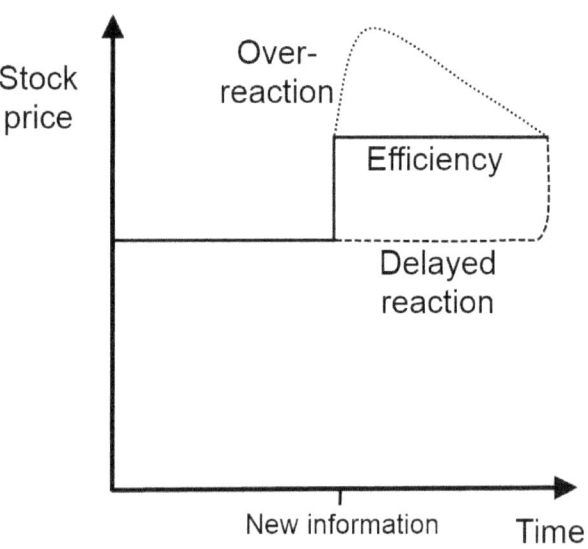

The diagram shows a situation where new information has become available which suggests that a stock price is worth more than previously thought. If the market is efficient then the stock market price would be expected to follow the solid line, and immediately increase a certain amount that reflects the exact change in value, before remaining at this new higher price. A slow delayed reaction to this new information as shown by the dashed line represents market inefficiency, as for a period the stock would be underpriced and investors could accurately predict a price rise, and they may buy it then and enjoy guaranteed excess returns. The highest dotted line also represents market inefficiency, and although there's a speedy and immediate reaction to the new information the reaction is of poor quality. At first it's an overreaction for a price that's too high, and then it's an underreaction as the movement to the correct price is gradual and not in one step. A firm could use this to rip off investors with misleading and excessive stock prices.

There are three forms of efficient market hypothesis:

Weak form: market prices reflect all of the information contained in past market prices;

Semi-strong form: market prices reflect all publicly available information;

Strong from: market prices reflect all available information, both public and private.

By definition the higher forms of market efficiency also include the lower forms, and if strong efficiency holds then semi-strong and weak form efficiency are also present. The following image gives a graphical representation of the relationship between the three forms.

Forms of the efficient market hypothesis

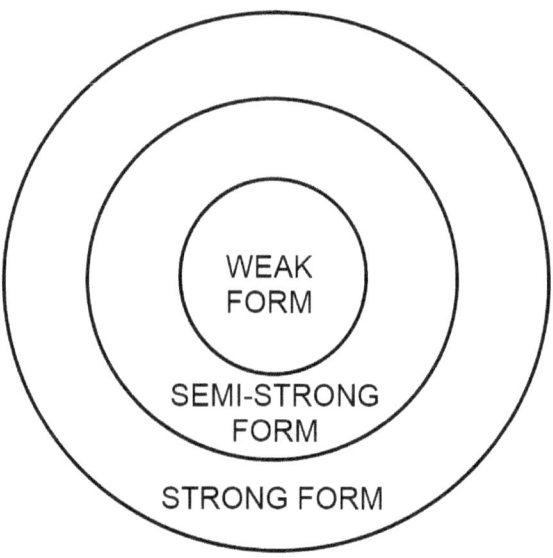

One way of looking at it is to say that weak form efficiency sees past information (past market prices) represented in current market prices; semi-strong form efficiency represents both current (public) and past information represented in prices; and strong form efficiency represents future (knowledge), current and past information in prices.

It's worth noting that market efficiency doesn't mean that picking stocks randomly will earn the same as a well diversified portfolio that reduces risk, nor that there can't be wild stock price fluctuations, or trends in past prices, that a lucky investor may be able to happen upon by chance. The EMH only suggests that any opportunities to earn excess returns will quickly disappear as they become known, and shared among increased numbers of attentive investors. It insists that the best and most reliable strategy for an investor is to combine the risk-free rate with a well diversified market portfolio, with the purchase of the market index.

5.2 Beating the Market

Despite the efficient market hypothesis (EMH) there are many who swear by market inefficiency, and insist that they have an active strategy to 'beat the market' and earn excess returns, outperforming the purely passive investment strategy of diversifying away risk and combining the market portfolio with the risk-free rate.

There are three different types of finance professionals who dedicate their focus to proving one of the three forms of market efficiency wrong:

Technical analysts (chartists) look for patterns and trends in historical price data, the existence of which would suggest that markets are weak form inefficient;

Fundamental analysts examine and assess publicly available data such as firm characteristics, announcements, press releases, and events, for their effect on assets. If fundamental analysts are successful in finding a correlation then that implies markets are semi-strong form inefficient;

Insider traders use information that is not yet available to the market but will have an impact in the future, such as hearing directly from the source that the director of a firm is planning to make changes that will transform its value. Insider traders suggest that markets are not strong form efficient.

If any of these methods are successful then the idea of market efficiency may be significantly weakened, and with it the essential role that the market plays in a well functioning modern economy. The robustness of the weak, semi-strong, and strong form EMH are therefore worth evaluation, and the next section looks into technical analysis, fundamental analysis, and insider trading in more detail. Various methods used to perform these alternative strategies are explained, and a range of academic literature and ideas are examined to assess the threat they pose to market efficiency.

5.3 Weak Form Market Analysis

If historical share prices do follow a random walk as the weak form efficient market hypothesis insists, then the price today, P_t, should be the price yesterday, P_{t-1}, with a random difference or error today, e_t:

$$P_t = P_{t-1} + e_t$$

And the correlation between these random differences or errors over time, known as serial correlation, should equal zero or they would not be random:

$$cor(e_t, e_{t-1}) = 0$$

Lo and MacKinlay (1999) find evidence of short-run serial correlations in stock prices, which they believe challenges the idea that market prices are random. Lo et al. (2000) also find predictable trends in stock prices, and argue that 'head and shoulders' patterns can be identified in the data they have examined, which could be capitalised on by investors.

Malkiel (2003) argues that statistical significance should be distinguished from economic significance, and that the researchers mentioned above have only found short-run momentum effects, which aren't significant or prolonged enough to allow investors to generate excess returns, especially after transaction costs and taxes are taken into account. He examines long-run serial correlation values and again finds support for the EMH as excess returns are not possible, and an investor is better off investing in the market index with a passive investment strategy. Fama and Blume (1966) examine the use of filter technical trading rules based on momentum trends in stock prices, and they also find no evidence that the market is inefficient. Their research finds that a passive buy-and-hold strategy using the market portfolio offers superior returns to use of a trading rule.

Brock et al. (1992) use trading rules where a buy or sell is made following changes in moving averages or a trading-range breakout, so called 'support and resistance', and find that this strategy offered excess returns over a buy-and-hold policy for U.S. DOW Jones securities for the years 1897-1986. The size of profits found is disputed by Bessembinder and Chan (1998) who point to measurement errors from non-synchronous trading, but they support the idea that general profits are made using the strategies. This may suggest that the market was inefficient in the distant past, but Ready (2002) updated the study for the years 1987-2002 and found poor performance from the trading rules. Perhaps the market was inefficient in the past but it appears to be far more efficient now going on this evidence.

There are also other studies that support the idea that the market has become more efficient over time. Olson (2004) examined 18 foreign exchange rates and concluded that the profits on offer with a simple moving average rule had fallen considerably, from roughly 3% in the late 1970s to almost nothing in the late 1990s.

Overall the academic theory suggests that the market is weak form efficient, and it isn't possible to use historical price data to forecast future prices and outperform the market index, after transaction costs and taxes are taken into account. But despite this there's a large professional following of technical analysis (TA), as financial analysts often use it as a central part of their business strategy. This is especially true over the short-term with time horizons of intraday or less than a week, and Taylor and Allen (1992) found this was popular with foreign exchange dealers in London, while Cheung and Wong (2000) confirmed the same in the Far East.

One explanation for practitioner usage of TA despite the theory of market efficiency may be the assumptions made, and it's usually assumed that investors are risk averse (i.e. they want to lower risk, as a loss hurts more than the potential of an equivalent gain), or at least risk neutral. But it's possible that those practicing TA may be risk seeking (i.e. they welcome risk, as a gain offers more than an equivalent loss hurts), and if this is the case then the well diversified market portfolio may not hold enough risk for them. Although selection of the market index with a passive buy-and-hold strategy may earn a low return with almost no effort, a risk seeking investor would prefer to risk a poor return and invest considerable effort to chase the chance, however small, of large returns. This is similar to someone buying a lottery ticket when the evidence shows that they're almost certainly waiting their money. Related to this is the issue of hubris, as investors or those acting on their behalf know that exploitable opportunities have existed in the past, and feel sure that their skill will see them achieved again.

Or perhaps the popularity of TA is simply an example of market efficiency in action. Fama (1965) noted that market efficiency comes about through competition among market participants, whose interest or lack of interest reveals new information about the value of assets and sees market prices adjust to a new level. Maintaining an efficient market would therefore require activity, competition and discovery of new information by investors, and what better way to ensure this than for investors to believe there are profits to be gained by intraday trading, based solely on recent past prices.

5.4 Semi-Strong Form Market Analysis

Semi-strong form market efficiency depends on the inability of investors to earn excess returns using any publicly available information. In an efficient market investors should be unable to earn excess returns by picking stocks based on known firm characteristics. But Fama and French (1992) show that so called 'value' stocks outperform 'growth' stocks, as stocks with low price-earnings multiples or low price-to-book-value ratios do better than stocks with higher values in these fields. This could allow the potential for investors to 'stock pick' for higher returns, and suggests market inefficiency. The authors are also among many who find that small firms typically outperform larger firms, which again could be exploited by investors.

Malkiel (2003) points out that the small firm and 'value' stock effects are likely to be time dependent, and although these anomalies may very well have existed in the past, there's evidence that profits can't be made using them today. Furthermore, any evidence that small firms outperform larger ones must take into account the effects of survivorship bias. It may be the case that small firms do worse than large ones overall, but a small firm that does poorly is likely to be unable to survive and its stock will simply disappear. A study of small vs. large firm stocks would therefore see the surviving best small firms vs. both the best and worst large firms, which will give misleading results. Fama and French (1996) also find that low price-to-book-value stocks are more prone to financial distress, and it may be the case that survivorship bias can help explain why value stocks appear to perform better too.

Even if firm size and book-to-market-value do have a major impact on firm value this doesn't prove market inefficiency according to Malkiel (2003). It may simply mean that the capital asset pricing model (CAPM) used to value stocks doesn't capture all aspects of risk. Fama and French (1993) argue in favour of a three factor model instead, combining the beta risk factor of the CAPM with additional factors for small capitalisation and high book-to-market-value.

While firm characteristics are a 'bottom up' way to perform fundamental analysis and test semi-strong form inefficiency, there is also a 'top down' method. This examines external factors to see whether the market represents all information before excess returns over the market rate are possible. Fama et al. (1969) look at event studies and the response to announcements, and find that the market correctly anticipates the price change and adjusts significantly before the announcement, with the rest of the change coming soon after. This is what would be expected in an efficient market, and this research paper was written in the late 1960s, before the period where the market is generally accepted to have become far more efficient, from the 1980s onwards.

An alternative top down way to perform fundamental analysis is to look for anomalies. One example of this is calendar effects where firms are thought to perform better or worse during different calendar dates. There is the day end, weekend, or holiday effect before the market closes for a period, the Monday effect when the market reopens, and seasonal effects such as the January effect where prices are thought to rise as investors try to minimize their income tax burden, or spend their end of year bonus on stocks.

Mehdian and Perry (2002) look specifically into the January effect using dummy variables, which isolates the effects of each of the twelve calendar months to see if the month makes any difference to returns. Over the period 1964-98 their results show that the individual months of January and April are statistically significant at the 5% significance level (i.e. 5% margin of error), to suggest that these months may have an effect on returns. But as noted earlier there's a difference between statistical significance and economic significance, and results only held up at the more stringent 1% significance level (1% margin of error) once, for one market index in January, which indicates that the calendar effects are not so reliable as to be certainties.

When Mehdian and Perry divided their sample period into two, a 1964-87 period and another for 1987-98, the results were transformed. The statistical significance was weaker all round, and the findings from the more recent time period 1987-98 suggests that calendar effects won't challenge market efficiency. Over 1987-98 the April calendar effect was only present with a 10% level of significance in most markets (10% margin of error), and indicates a more efficient market in recent decades. Meanwhile the January effect disappeared completely, to be replaced by a December effect at the 5% significance level. With the month offering excess returns changing over time, and only present with notable margins of error, it is unlikely that calendar effect anomalies would allow market beating returns after transaction costs are considered.

5.5 Strong Form Market Analysis

Strong form efficiency is a more difficult area to find research, as researchers don't usually have access to insider information to be able to judge its effects. Unlike other forms of the efficient market hypothesis no-one is likely to voluntarily reveal detailed information on insider trading as the practice is illegal, and anyone linked to it could find themselves in jail.

But it's safe to assume that those with inside information on a firm's future could exploit it. They could predict price rises and buy stock (going long in finance terms), if they knew a lucrative merger was forthcoming, or foresee price falls and sell off stocks with the intention of buying back at a lower price (going short), if they knew that the respected CEO was about to leave for a rival. Although other investors would soon pick up on the trends, seeing profits divided among many and disappearing to nothing, profits may still be on offer for the original investor whose inside knowledge puts him a step ahead. However, there are two problems with this. The first is that if the insider trader has access to private information of value then it's likely that others will too, and they could make it public before the insider trader has the chance to exploit it. The second issue is transaction costs again removing market index beating returns, and this doesn't just mean the monetary cost of trades and capital gains tax, but the cost of huge fines and jail time if the insider trade was to be discovered.

Just like the weak and semi-strong form market efficiency, strong form appears to have flaws that may be exploitable. But these don't necessarily appear to be reliable for an investor, and it may be that the market isn't perfectly inefficient but efficient enough to do its job, yet also inefficient enough so that investors believe they can beat it, thereby seeing them constantly work and uncover new information which keeps the market efficient and functional in the process.

Bibliography

Ang, A. and Chen, J. (2007) CAPM Over the Long-Run: 1926-2001, *Journal of Empirical Finance*, Vol. 14, No. 1, pp.1-40.

Bessembinder, H. and Chan, K. (1998) Market Efficiency and the Returns to Technical Analysis, *Financial Management*, Vol. 27, No. 2, pp.5-17.

Black, F. (1993) Beta and Return, *Journal of Portfolio Management*, Vol. 20, pp.8-18.

Brock, W., Lakonishok, J. and LeBaron, B. (1992) Simple Technical Trading Rules and the Stochastic Properties of Stock Returns, *Journal of Finance*, Vol. 47, No. 5, pp.1731-64.

Chan, L. K. C., and Lakonishok, J. (1993) Are the Reports of Beta's Death Premature? *Journal of Portfolio Management*, Vol. 19, pp.51-62.

Cheung, Y. -W. and Wong, C. Y. -P. (2000) A Survey of Market Practitioners' Views On Exchange Rate Dynamics,

Journal of International Economics, Vol. 51, No. 2, pp.401-19.

Davis, J., Fama, E., and French, K. (2000) Characteristics, Covariances, and Average Returns: 1929 to 1997, *The Journal of Finance*, Vol. 55, No. 1, pp.389-406.

Fama, E. (1965) Random Walks In Stock Prices, *Financial Analysts Journal*, Vol. 21, No. 5, p.56.

Fama, E. and Blume, M. (1966) Filter Rules and Stock Market Trading Profits, *Journal of Business*, Vol. 39, pp.226-41.

Fama, E. and MacBeth, J. (1973) Risk, Return and Equilibrium: Empirical Tests, *The Journal of Political Economy*, Vol. 81, No.3, pp.607-36.

Fama, E., Fisher, L., Jensen, M. C., and Roll, R. (1969) The Adjustment of Stock Prices to New Information, *International Economic Review*, Vol. 10, No. 1, pp.1-21.

Fama, E. and French, K. (1992) The Cross-Section Of Expected Stock Returns, *Journal of Finance*, Vol. 47, No. 2, pp.427-65.

Fama, E. and French, K. (1993) Common Risk Factors in the Returns on Stocks and Bonds, *Journal of Financial Economics*, Vol. 33, No. 1, pp.3-56.

Fama, E. and French, K. (1996) Multifactor Explanations of Asset Pricing Anomalies, *Journal of Finance*, Vol. 51, No. 1, pp.55-84.

Hsia, C-C., Fuller, B. R., and Chen, B. Y. J. (2000) Is Beta Dead or Alive? *Journal of Business Finance and Accounting*, Vol. 27, No.3-4, pp.283-311.

Kandel, S. and Stambaugh, R. F. (1995) Portfolio Inefficiency and the Cross-Section of Expected Returns, *Journal of Finance*, Vol. 50, pp.157-84.

Kendall, M. G. and Bradford Hill, A. (1953) The Analysis of Economic Time-Series Part I: Prices, *Journal of the Royal Statistical Society, Series A* (Blackwell Publishing), Vol. 116, No. 1, pp.11-34.

Kothari, S. P., Shanken, J. and Sloan, R. G. (1995) Another Look at the Cross-Section of Expected Returns, *Journal of Finance*, Vol. 50, pp.185-224.

Lo, A. W. and MacKinlay A. C. (1999) *A Non-Random Walk Down Wall Street*, Princeton: Princeton University Press.

Lo, A. W., Mamaysky, H., and Wang, J. (2000) Foundations of Technical Analysis: Computational Algorithms, Statistical Inference, and Empirical Implementation, *Journal of Finance*, Vol. 55, No. 4, pp.1705-765.

Malkiel, B. G. (2003) The Efficient Market Hypothesis and Its Critics, *Journal of Economic Perspectives*, Vol. 17, No. 1, pp.59-82.

Mehdian, S. and Perry, M. J. (2002) Anomalies in U.S. Equity Markets: A Re-examination of the January Effect, *Applied Financial Economics*, Vol. 12, pp.141-45.

Olson, D. (2004) Have Trading Rule Profits In The Currency Markets Declined Over Time? *Journal of Banking and Finance*, Vol. 28, pp.85-105.

Ready, M. J. (2002) Profits from Technical Trading Rules, *Financial Management*, Vol. 31, No. 3, pp.43-61.

Roll, R. (1977) A Critique of the Asset Pricing Theory's Tests Part I: On Past and Potential Testability of the Theory, *Journal of Financial Economics*, Vol. 4, No. 2, pp.129-76.

Ross, S. (1976) The Arbitrage Theory of Capital Asset Pricing, *Journal of Economic Theory*, Vol. 13, No. 3, pp.341-60.

Taylor, M. P., and Allen, H. (1992) The Use of Technical Analysis in the Foreign Exchange Market, *Journal of International Money and Finance*, Vol. 11, No. 3, pp.304-14.

Tobin, J. (1958) Liquidity Preference As Behaviour Towards Risk, *The Review Of Economic Studies*, Oxford: Oxford University Press, Vol. 25, No. 2, pp.65-86.

www.ingramcontent.com/pod-product-compliance
Lightning Source LLC
Chambersburg PA
CBHW051732170526
45167CB00002B/906